Jim Henson

Muppet Master

Jim Henson

Muppet Master

Nathan Aaseng

Lerner Publications Company
Minneapolis

To Danielle and Devin

Photo credits:
Cover photographs by Nancy Moran/Sygma
Phototeque, pp. 1, 9, 17, 18, 32, 36; Nancy Moran/Sygma, pp. 2-3;
Frank Edwards/Pictorial Parade, p. 6; Gary Gershoff/Retna
Ltd., p. 10; TV Times, p. 12; Danny Chin/Star File, pp. 22, 23;
Mike Grossman/Globe Photo, p. 24; Larry White/Retna Ltd.,
p. 26; Vinnie Zuffante/Star File, p. 30; Tri-Star Pictures Inc., p. 35

Manufactured in the United States of America

LIBRARY OF CONGRESS CATALOGING-IN-PUBLICATION DATA

Aaseng, Nathan.
    Jim Henson: Muppet master/Nathan Aaseng.
      p. cm.

    Summary: Recounts how Jim Henson brought to life the Muppets and
how he made other advances in the world of puppetry.
    ISBN 0-8225-1615-2 (lib. bdg.)
    1. Henson, Jim—Juvenile literature. 2. Muppet show (Television
program)—Juvenile literature. 3. Television producers and
directors—United States—Biography—Juvenile literature. 4. Muppet
show (Television program) [1. Henson, Jim. 2. Television
producers and directors. 3. Puppets.] I. Title.
PN1982.H46A62 1988
791.5'3'0924—dc19
[B]
[92]
                                                                                        87-23262
                                                                                        CIP
                                                                                        AC

1 2 3 4 5 6 7 8 9 10 98 97 96 95 94 93 92 91 90 89 88

Contents

6

A Coat
Comes to Life

To the average person, it may have looked like nothing more than a worn-out green overcoat. But Jim Henson saw something else in his mother's old coat. With a few minor adjustments and a couple of Ping-Pong balls for eyes, it began to take the shape of a new celebrity. Borrowing the name of an old schoolboy chum from Mississippi, Kermit Scott, Henson had all the raw material he needed. Somehow, with just a few flutters of his fingers, Henson brought that material to life as one of the most popular entertainers in the world, Kermit the Frog.

Jim Henson has an almost magical skill: he turns cloth and plastic into lovable, *real* characters. Because of this ability, he has been called the Walt Disney of his generation. Starting as a one-man operation, Henson

Associates has mushroomed into a multi-million dollar business employing well over 100 workers. It has cranked out hundreds of cloth and plastic foam "Muppets" who appear in TV shows, motion pictures, cartoons, and on countless pieces of merchandise in stores. The names Miss Piggy, Big Bird, Oscar the Grouch, Fozzie, Gonzo, and dozens more are recognized throughout the world.

More important to Henson, however, these characters have broken many of the barriers of show business. Before the Muppets came along, puppets were rarely taken seriously as a means of entertainment. Network executives echoed the common feeling that only small children could be taken in by the simple, primitive world of make-believe in which puppets live. Henson knew better. He created such warm, appealing personalities for his Muppets that adults as well as children could identify with them.

The Muppets' hold over their audience has been so strong that even skeptics have been won over. Largely because of the enthusiastic backing of adult viewers, "The Muppet Show" became the most successful syndicated show ever produced. The great comedian Bob Hope said that working with the Muppets "drove me up a wall" at first. But his discomfort at being "a stooge for their antics" quickly melted away and he ended up "loving it." Morley Safer tried to interview the Muppets for a segment of the news show "60 Minutes." He found himself laughing uncontrollably at their nonsense.

Entertainers Lily Tomlin and Paul Williams both expressed an empty feeling about not being able to go out for coffee with the Muppets between scenes, as they would with other actors.

Not content with creating lifelike characters, Henson has gone on to create lifelike worlds. He has taken the art of puppetry further than anyone dreamed it could go. Yet the tall, bearded Muppet master keeps looking for ways to take it ever further. Jim Henson is a creative explorer probing the limits of what puppets can accomplish.

Henson created an entirely new world in the movie _Dark Crystal._ Here the Gelfling, Jen, plays a flute as Kira sings along.

Lured into Television

It has been said of James Maury Henson that most experiences in his life turn up in a Muppet personality. If that is true, then the Muppets began with Henson's birth on September 24, 1936, in Greenville, Mississippi. His father's job as an agricultural research biologist put him in the quiet of the countryside. It was a simple world, much like the innocent world of the Muppets. Jim could ride horses through the fields and fish in a creek that ran through his front yard. A poor athlete, he found enjoyment in drawing, painting, and cartooning, rather than in sports.

As a child, he never owned a puppet and never wanted to. But there were some influences from the puppet world. As an eight-year-old, he listened to radio broadcasts of Edgar Bergen, a ventriloquist who used a

Charlie McCarthy and Edgar Bergen performing on stage

dummy named Charlie McCarthy. Jim never thought of
Charlie as a puppet, however. To him, Charlie was a
real person. After moving to suburban Washington, D.C.,
in the fifth grade, Henson begged his parents to buy a
television. He nearly drove them crazy with his pleading
until they finally gave in.

Some of his parents' doubts about television came true when, as a teenager, Jim was the next thing to a TV junkie. Among the shows he watched was "Kukla, Fran, and Ollie," in which a human conversed with puppets. Bill and Cora Baird also appeared on TV, working their marionettes (puppets operated by strings instead of by a hand inside them). But these were just two interesting shows that happened to be on television. It was TV that fascinated Henson, not puppets.

Then in the summer of 1954, a local television show advertised that they were holding tryouts for a new puppet show. Although he didn't know much about puppets, Henson was thrilled at the idea of being involved with television. He and a friend built a rat puppet and a couple of cowboy puppets and put together an act. The newcomer's performance earned him a job on "The Junior Morning Show." His beginner's luck seemed to run out, however, as the show was canceled after only three weeks.

Fortunately, NBC network executives happened to be watching and they liked Henson's style. They hired him as a puppeteer to help out on a cartoon show. Having found such instant success, Henson enrolled in a puppeteering course at the University of Maryland. He also studied acting, staging, and scene design. As fast as he learned new techniques, he was called upon to use them. By the end of his freshman year, 1955, Henson had his own show. Two five-minute time slots were

13

reserved at night for his "Sam and His Friends," which starred a bald, bug-eyed puppet. Working with another University of Maryland puppetry student, Jane Nebel, Henson constructed a supporting cast of puppets, including a frog-like creature named Kermit.

"Sam and His Friends" used only visual gimmicks—the puppets didn't speak. But when Henson signed on to do a series of commercials for Wilkins coffee, he was asked to add dialogue to his act. From the beginning, Henson realized that television and puppets were a special mix. The TV camera could be selective in what it showed, so that the puppeteer could be more easily kept out of sight. But it also could bring the audience much closer to the puppets. That meant that great care needed to be taken in synchronizing mouth movements to the dialogue. Henson brought a TV monitor behind the scenes with him while he worked so that he could see exactly what the audience was seeing. This method, and the technique of mouthing only the important syllables of a sentence, have become Muppet trademarks.

Henson's coffee commercials (all 160 of them) were so successful that he was bombarded with awards and offers. In 1957 he appeared on Steve Allen's "Tonight Show" on national TV. Kermit the Frog, dressed in a blond wig, sang "I've Grown Accustomed to Your Face" to a purple monster. The monster, operated by Jane Nebel, promptly ate his own face and then attacked poor Kermit, who was operated by Henson.

14

For a while, Henson's puppetry career was going great. He was allowed to experiment with all kinds of off-beat humor and creative ideas on his show. It paid for a Rolls-Royce to drive him to his college graduation and let him plan a trip to Europe. But after college he figured he would quit. He was a married man (to Jane Nebel in 1959), and playing around with puppets was not the type of thing a grown man did for a living.

But his European travels changed his mind. In Europe, the craft of puppetry was appreciated as an art form. Henson saw that puppets could be more than kid stuff. He returned home determined to make it his life's work to advance the art of puppetry in the United States.

The Muppet master had no master plan for doing that, however. "I never planned my career," he says. It was just a matter of doing what seemed correct, and one thing leading to another. This "build as you go" attitude that later drove some of his associates crazy may be best illustrated by the name of his act, "The Muppets." For years Henson explained that the word was a combination of "marionette" and "puppet" that helped describe his creations. It wasn't until nearly thirty years after his act had started that he finally admitted that he had only been giving people the kind of logical answer they were expecting. In fact, "muppet" was just a name he pulled out of the air that somehow seemed to fit.

Henson had many qualities that helped him steer his

way to success. Among these was a willingness to try new methods. For example, most European puppeteers used wood in building their puppets. Although wooden puppets were sturdy and worked well for live performances, they lacked flexibility. Henson saw that in order to come alive under the close-up gaze of television, his puppets would have to be more elastic. Some of his puppets were little more than elaborate socks and others were made of pliable plastic foam.

Equally important to the success of the Muppets was Henson's eye for talent. Now that the Muppets were taking on speaking roles, Jane Henson did not feel comfortable as a performer. With the birth of their first child in 1960, the Hensons were ready for her to leave the business and devote more effort to raising a family. But it would be difficult to replace her talent. At a National Puppet Convention in 1961, Jim met a team of puppeteers that especially impressed him. He immediately asked one of them, Jerry Juhl, to join him as a puppeteer. The other was a boy of seventeen named Frank Oz. Although Henson could not hire such a young person, he kept close tabs on Oz. When Oz was ready for full-time work three years later, Henson hired him. He then asked Juhl to concentrate his talents on script-writing. Henson freely gives credit to these two for bringing a spark of humor and professionalism to the Muppets.

Gradually the Muppets began to slip into brief spots

In 1973, Jim Henson appeared on "The Dick Cavett Show" with the Muppet Jim.

on national networks. A floppy-eared, piano-playing dog named Rowlf was recruited as a regular on the country-western flavored "Jimmy Dean Show" from 1963 to 1966. The Muppets even made appearances on the popular "Ed Sullivan Show," surviving the indignity of being introduced once as "Jim Jensen and the Moffets."

Recovery from Success

The big break that made certain such a slip would never happen again came in 1969. That year Henson was asked to create characters for the new Public Broadcasting Station's children's show, "Sesame Street." Henson and his crew built characters for the show in their usual gradual way. Instead of designing a character around a real person, they started with a few simple personality traits or attitudes. For instance, they wanted a character who could help children learn from childish mistakes. This would have to be a larger-than-life character to make the mistakes obvious and out in the open, yet very childlike so that children could identify with its actions. Instead of a regular puppet, they created an eight-foot-tall bird operated by a person inside it, now known as Big Bird. By the end of the first season, Henson's new cast of characters had won an enthusiastic audience. The Count, Cookie Monster, Fozzie Bear, Bert and Ernie, and Grover quickly won the hearts of a generation of young Americans. Henson's constant fine-tuning of his characters and attention to quality earned many awards as well. In 1974, the Muppets won another television industry Emmy Award, this time for "outstanding achievement in the field of children's programming."

Yet the runaway success of the "Sesame Street" Muppets actually dealt a dangerous blow to Henson's career. The Muppets became strongly identified with preschool children. When Henson tried to persuade major networks to give him a weekly variety series aimed at families, they wouldn't consider it. The popularity of "Sesame Street" reinforced the "obvious fact" that puppets were kid stuff. Although the networks admired Henson's work, all their offers included the one condition that the show be geared for small children. The years he had spent trying to show that puppets could be more than entertainment for small children seemed wasted.

Fortunately for Henson, one wealthy English businessman believed his arguments. Lord Lew Grade offered to put up the money to produce the show if Henson would come to London to film it. Lord Grade would then sell the show to independent stations around the world. In 1976, Henson and his team arrived in

London to take up the challenge. One of the most difficult problems was finding guest stars to appear on the show. Henson did not have lots of money to offer celebrities, who were already suspicious about appearing on a puppet show that they were almost certain would fail. It was important that "The Muppet Show" quickly build a good reputation.

Again, Henson had no master plan for "The Muppet Show" to follow. He relied on his instincts and discovered what would work as he went along. He did not let pride stand in his way. If a character or a routine seemed to be floundering, Henson could immediately make sweeping changes or drop the idea altogether. For example, he started out using a character named Nigel the Bandleader as the host of his show. Henson quickly sensed that Nigel wasn't giving the show quite the flavor it needed. So the Muppet master turned to one of his oldest creations, Kermit the Frog. Kermit had been a minor character in and out of Henson sketches for almost twenty years. Now he proved to be just the solid personality needed to make the show work.

Other members of Henson's team displayed the same instincts for making the right changes. An early production number called for a chorus of animals. Although there were no plans to use these puppets on a regular basis, one of the pigs seemed special to puppeteer Frank Oz. Gradually he shaped the personality of the vain, desperately-in-search-of-stardom Miss Piggy. Jane

Henson once said that Frank and Jim were good partners because Oz tended to overact while Henson tended to underdo a part. The controlled Kermit and the outrageous Miss Piggy formed an unbeatable team.

A few brave souls, such as actress Candice Bergen (who was familiar with puppets, being the daughter of Edgar Bergen), led the way as Muppet guests. They

Miss Piggy gets a costume change and a check of hair and makeup by a group of attendants on the set.

Filming *The Muppets Take Manhattan*, Frank Oz (in glasses) prepares to bring Miss Piggy alive for the cameras.

passed on the word that "The Muppet Show" was something special. "It's organized by the most professional group of people imaginable," said Hal Linden, TV's Barney Miller.

Henson came up with a unique way of putting his guests at ease in the world of puppetry. Each guest was brought into a meeting room where he or she met with Henson and his associates. As they spoke about their ideas for the show, Muppet characters gradually appeared and joined in the conversation. Before long the guest would be chatting with them as though they were real people. By the end of the meeting, most guests were totally enchanted by their new friends. Most could hardly believe the Muppets were just cloth and plaster. Even Henson and his friends got so caught up in the characters that they found it hard to break out of their roles. Offstage, Kermit and his friends would be clowning around while the pigs pounded each other in a full-scale brawl.

In 1986, Kermit and Scooter (assisted by Jim Henson and Richard Hunt) presented the Oscar for best animated short film to the film's director, Cilia Van Dijk.

24

As the show's popularity grew, it became a status symbol for a star to appear on the show. Such diverse people as George Burns, Raquel Welch, Orson Welles, Christopher Reeve, and Alice Cooper joined in the fun. Still, there was no question who were the real stars of the show. In 1977 actress Rita Moreno won an Emmy Award for an appearance on "The Muppet Show." Although she was the only human who appeared on camera, her award was for "outstanding *supporting* actress."

Rarely has anyone proven the "experts" wrong as convincingly as Henson's Muppets did. By 1978 the show had attracted an estimated 230 million viewers in 106 countries. Best of all, it was not just children who tuned into the show. When "The Muppet Show" was moved to a children's time slot in England for 1977, a deafening howl of protest from adults forced programmers to put it back where it had been. In the United States the family puppet show gained an audience of 40 million, making it the most successful syndicated show in the country's history. Surveys showed that three of every four viewers were adults. Perhaps the most satisfying achievement for Henson in advancing the cause of puppetry came in 1978. "The Muppet Show" was named by the television industry "the outstanding comedy, variety, or musical series" on the air. Not the outstanding *children's* series, the outstanding *series*.

The Invisible Man

Despite his success, Jim Henson remained so invisible that he was doing credit card commercials highlighting the fact that when he traveled, "people didn't know him." In fact, the ability to keep himself and his operators out of the picture may have been one of the most important keys to his success. Henson once said that he never wanted the audience to think "How do they do that?" or "Isn't that clever how they managed that trick?" He wanted the audience to be so drawn to the character that they didn't notice the behind-the-scenes manipulation at all.

Keeping the puppeteers out of the picture was especially difficult during some of the Muppets' larger musical numbers. Henson worked with about fifteen basic types of puppets, each of which was operated in a different way. The simplest of these were hand puppets, such as Kermit. Henson, working below the stage, spoke for and operated this master of ceremonies. One hand went inside Kermit's head while the other hand manuevered the strings, rods, and other controls that moved his tiny arms. The strings were painted the color of the background so they would not be visible.

More complex puppets such as Miss Piggy (who can hold objects in her hands) required two operators. Frank Oz controlled Piggy's head with one hand and one of her arms with the other, while another puppeteer moved her other arm. All of the puppeteers watched a television monitor below the stage so they could see what the audience saw.

It was no easy matter to have five puppeteers crawling around beneath the stage, trying to keep out of each other's way without fouling up strings or rods and knocking over monitors. Yet the viewer never had the slightest clue of the chaos that existed just inches away from the camera.

What the audience saw was a tribute to the puppeteers' art. Except for opening and closing a Muppet's mouth and tilting its head, there was no way to change its expression. Yet Henson and his crew could get across what his strange-looking creations were feeling. With the tiniest shift of the head position or the slightest change in the angle of the mouth opening, they could make a puppet appear sad or happy or frustrated, or any of dozens of other emotions.

The puppets also had an advantage in the fact that they could do things that ordinary humans couldn't. They could get blown up or wiped out in an avalanche without feeling any pain. They could say outrageous things that humans would be too polite to say.

To everyone around him, Henson's life must have seemed hectic. He had to juggle the demands of his career, spending six months of the year in London, with his role as father of five children in New York. Jim helped ease this problem by allowing his children to help in Muppet productions. Meanwhile, the problem of keeping control over the frenzy on the set of "The Muppet Show" didn't bother him the way it would most people. The drive to create was too strong to allow him to live a slower-paced, more orderly life.

In the words of a guest star, actor Christopher Reeve, Henson "knew absolutely what he was doing." As an example, while "The Muppet Show" was at the height of its success, Henson turned off its cameras for good. It had only been on the air five years. After 120 shows, each of which had used the same theme—a group of crazy individuals struggling to put on a performance— Henson sensed that the show would soon lose its freshness. Rather than wait until that happened, Henson moved on to other, more ambitious projects.

A World
from Scratch

It had been a stroke of genius to bring celebrities from real life into the world of the Muppets. Henson had long wondered what would happen if he tried to do the opposite. Could he take his Muppets off the stage and into the real world? Henson decided that he could use motion pictures to try.

With hard work, many creative experiments, and eight million dollars, Henson and his crew made *The Muppet Movie*. In writing his movie, he relied on his basic philosophy of life. "We use a positive approach," he often said. "We say that life is good, that people are good." In a Muppet version of a standard plot, the unknown country frog, Kermit, rises out of the Georgia swamps to overcome evil and gain wealth and fame.

Henson takes to the water to prepare for Kermit's guitar-playing scene in *The Muppet Movie.* **A couple of assistants stand by to help.**

As an illustration of the creativity used to solve problems that seemed impossible, the opening scene called for Kermit to play his guitar in a swamp setting. True to his goal of bringing puppets into the real world, Henson refused to settle for a stage decorated like a swamp. Instead he crawled into an airtight tank and had it lowered into the water. Then a log was placed over the tank. Breathing air fed into the tank, he operated Kermit through a sealed sleeve at the top of the tank. Since Henson's hands could operate only the head and the strumming arm, another technician controlled the

32

other hand electronically from shore. The cameras recorded the astounding picture of a puppet playing and singing in the middle of a real swamp, complete with guitar fingering for chord changes! Always concerned about details, Henson had his tank equipped with TV monitors so he could watch his performance. Divers stood by to rescue him in case anything went wrong.

Such technical innovations combined with the familiar Muppet personalities to make *The Muppet Movie* another Henson breakthrough. His instincts seemed to always point toward success. *The Great Muppet Caper* and *The Muppets Take Manhattan* delighted film critics as well as fans. Two new television series got off the ground in the early 1980s. The cartoon series "The Muppet Babies" took advantage of the familiar "Muppet Show" characters to enter the children's Saturday morning television world. Meanwhile, a whole new series of characters was created for the pay-TV show, "Fraggle Rock."

Henson found more new possibilities waiting as well. Whereas *The Muppet Movie* had once seemed the ultimate challenge, Henson now had a much larger challenge to work on. Backed by $20 million from his longtime supporter, Lord Grade, Henson plunged into the task of creating an entire world from scratch. For his new movie there would be no actors, no locations, no stages. Everything that existed in this puppet world would be born out of the imagination of Jim Henson and his company.

Starting with some designs by Englishman Brian Froud, author of a book called *Faeries*, Henson carefully created this new world. Ideas became pictures and pictures became three-dimensional. Since much of what he was doing had never been done before, he constantly had to invent new methods of making things move. With radio controls and electronic gadgets directing their movements, Henson's puppets sometimes were the next thing to robots. Henson again used a simple tale of good and evil to breathe life into his puppet world. After five years of work as the creator, co-director, and co-producer of the project, he presented *The Dark Crystal* to the public.

Those expecting the warm coziness which had delighted so many Muppet fans in other projects were stunned by this entirely new approach. *The Dark Crystal's* world held too much terror for preschool children to handle. "The Muppet Show" had shown that puppetry could appeal to the small child in adults. Now Henson had taken puppetry a step further to make a world that was beyond the reach of small children.

His film was admired as the "state of the art" in animated characters. *The Dark Crystal* helped open the gates for others to experiment with a flood of special effects efforts. A new generation of animation specialists followed Henson's footsteps. Within a few years after

David Bowie (left) was the star of *Labyrinth*, another movie for which Henson created an entirely new world.

the release of *The Dark Crystal*, there seemed to be no limit to what puppetry and its adaptations could do. Frank Oz used his experience with the Muppets to create special effects such as Yoda in *Star Wars* and to direct *The Little Shop of Horrors*.

Chip Off the Old Frog

Not since Walt Disney had one man's dreams created such an entertainment empire as Jim Henson has done with his Muppets. He has let his characters shine under the spotlight and it has been difficult to get past the puppets to find out who Jim Henson really is. Fortunately, according to his employees, there is a large clue that helps in understanding him. They say that if you gave Kermit the Frog a man's body, he would remind you very much of Jim Henson.

Kermit as been described as the "warm, solid thing in the middle" of the Muppets. Although frequently driven to frustration by the lunatic antics of those around him, he remains in control. Everyone else can panic when disaster after disaster overtakes them. But

Kermit somehow hangs on to his sanity and finds a way to get the job done.

Henson's workers say that this describes him well. Because of the demands of their hectic schedule and the many challenges they accept, Henson Associates often seems to face impossible situations. Jim just strolls about, peacefully taking care of details, and everything comes together just fine in the end.

When Kermit is in charge of the other Muppets, he does not dominate them. He accepts their contributions to the effort. In many ways a soft touch, he is easy to work for. Yet he is the boss. Jim Henson says, "We work as a team and have a good time working." His employees love working with him and see him as a caring, patient person. He freely gives people such as Frank Oz credit for the Muppets' success. Yet no one doubts that Henson has the final say in the creative side of the business.

Kermit is a frog of simple tastes. He's not out looking for the fame, status, and high living that Miss Piggy craves. After his fling with the Rolls-Royce in college, Henson seems to have walked the same path as Kermit. His idea of a good time is reading a book or being with his family in his Bedford, New York, home.

In "The Muppet Show" Kermit was bothered by a character named J.P. Gross who was always looking to sell out the show, grab the money, and run. Henson could easily have made a quick fortune on his early fame and coasted on it. But like Kermit, Henson was more interested in making the show work. He repeatedly funneled his profits back into the company so that they would be able to entertain people even better.

Although he has a strong sense of what is right, Kermit does not moralize or lecture. Henson's productions generally stay away from preaching loud, obvious messages. Instead, the messages come across in the humor and the attitudes of the characters. Mel Brooks says that their subtle message is that "the meek shall inherit the earth." They avoid politics and lightly poke fun at greed, selfishness, and narrowness. Henson's 1985 film, *Labyrinth*, strayed from this policy of the light touch and it seemed to cause him problems. He was concerned that children's programming was teaching kids that the key to peace and well-being was in destroying evil. He showed in the film that things weren't that simple. The film, starring rock star David Bowie, proved Henson's instincts weren't perfect. Although critics again admired his technical feats, many dismissed *Labyrinth* as a good idea that didn't work.

Finally, Kermit usually looks on the bright side of life. He's an honest, decent, average sort of guy who likes to find the good in others. Many think that it is because Kermit is so human, and maybe just a touch better, that people are drawn to like him so much. According to his employees, all of this would describe Henson perfectly.

Henson agrees that there is something of himself in Kermit. But Kermit is far more than just Henson's double. Those who spend time around Henson say that it isn't until he puts Kermit on his arm that he becomes witty and funny. Henson agrees that he would never say many of the things Kermit spouts from time to time. Having a puppet on his arm frees him to do things he ordinarily couldn't do. It has taken him a long time to help the rest of us realize that this is what puppets are for—to be characters just like us, who can do a little more than we can. They can show us things we couldn't see without them.

Jim Henson has shown us such a gift is not just for children. Comedian Steve Martin was speaking for adults as well as children when he once observed, exaggerating only slightly, "Pretty soon you don't want to talk to people any more. You just want to talk to the Muppets."